T0171666

ABC's

TO

HAPPINESS

FARRAH D. MCBRIDE

authorHOUSE®

AuthorHouse™
1663 Liberty Drive
Bloomington, IN 47403
www.authorhouse.com
Phone: 1 (800) 839-8640

Published by AuthorHouse   02/29/2016

ISBN: 978-1-5049-8013-5 (sc)
ISBN: 978-1-5049-8059-3 (e)

Library of Congress Control Number: 2016903450

Print information available on the last page.

CONTENTS

Thanks to my creator above for giving me the desire to write and share my gift with the world. Nothing in life is impossible for those that believe. If you believe it. You can achieve it. If you dream it can become a reality. To my son Zaiden, I love you. You are an extension of me, so your faith doesn't surprise me. Thanks for having faith in me when mine was wavering. To my family and friends, thanks for your love and support.

This book is dedicated to my mother who recently passed away. She was feisty, strong and full of faith. My mother gave me the most precious gift that anyone could ever give. She introduced me to Christ, which made me into the woman that I am today. Thanks Mom you are truly missed but never forgotten. This book is being written in one on the most traumatic times in my life. My mother who I loved passed away 11 Oct 2014. I could have allow time affect me, grieve and go into a deep depression, but I choose not. I choose to be happy. I chose life over death. Nothing or no one could ever replace her; knowing this, I stay strong in my faith in the Lord. I know that she is in a better place. She is doing all the things that she wanted and loved to do. Most importantly, I know she would want me to be happy and share with you what's on my heart and that will be the ABC's to a Happiness.

FIRST THINGS FIRST

"WORDS HAVE POWER"

Many of us have heard the expression that Actions speak louder than words. I grew up hearing this cliché and for the record it is one of the biggest fabrications ever told. The other one sticks and stones my break my bones, but words will never hurt me. What a bunch of monkey shine. Words do hurt. The words that we speak cause a reaction in that natural and the supernatural. Genesis 1: 1" God said, Let there be light and light was." This is so key. God didn't see light and say light be. He called it into existence. Light exists because he spoke out of his mouth. "Let there be light." Now we have gotten this out of the way, are you ready to learn your ABC's?

ASK

"CLOSED MOUTHS DON'T GET FED"

Happiness is not achieved by someone arbitrarily giving you things and or doing things for you because they think it would make you happy. You may not like, want or even accept everything that comes your way. Frankly if you are doing that then you are probably not very jubilant. Something simple we forget, because we are often afraid of how will be perceived is to simply ask. Let it be known what you want. Don't worry about being a people pleaser. You have to do and know what makes you happy, be vocal about it. You have not because you ask not. While you are reading this I challenge you to be honest about what you want. This is the first step into being happy.

Acknowledge that you have a right to be happy. Ask yourself, am I happy with a certain situation or relationship? After doing so, be bold; voice your concerns to about that situation or relationship. After doing so, ask yourself is this making me happy, or it causing me unnecessary stress and making me unhappy?

BELIEVE

"BELIEVING IN YOURSELF IS ONLY THE HALF OF IT"

You are probably saying believe. As if what is she talking about? Yes, I mean believe. You have to believe that you deserve to be happy and that it is okay, for someone else has to have a problem with what makes you happy. No one has to like what you like. The only person that has control over your happiness is you. You are the determining factor. So, what you are you going to do you? Are you going to express what it is that will make you happy, believe that you can receive it and see it become your reality. Or are you going to continue in your own self-pity and feel like you deserve whatever happens? The worst thing that anyone can ever do, and a sure recipe to unhappiness; is not knowing that you deserve to be happy. I remember while I was in the military. I met older women in her 50s. She never been married. However, she dated a married man. The two of them had dated him for 30 years. I asked her why she stayed, her response "I loved him." This puzzled me a beautiful, yet attractive older women stayed with a man for so long knowing that she would never be his wife. So I asked her, did you ever want to get married? She said. "Yes once." When the relationship ended, she lost the desire to ever want to get married. She believed that she did not deserve it.

I shared this to say. You don't have to settle and ever convince yourself that you don't deserve to be happy because of your past. You learn to let go of your past, so that you can grab hold of what is purposed for you. Let go and know what makes you happy and believe that your deserve it.

CARES

"IF YOU CAN'T CHANGE IT, WHY ARE YOU WORRYING ABOUT IT?"

As you are reading this, what is on your mind? What is worrying you, if anything? If so why is it? Can you change it by being so caught up in it? We all know the answer to that. Many times people put too much time into caring and worrying about things that they cannot change. You become stressed out, unhappy, unmotivated, your health declines. All this because you are busy worrying about the wrong things. Cast aside those cares, put away those things that weigh you down. People can weigh you down, and circumstances can weigh you down. If a situation you are caring and worrying about is not going to uplift you, encourage you, and or bring you to another level, then you need to let that monkey shine go. It isn't worth it. No one thing is worth you getting so caught up in it that it makes you unhappy.

DOUBT/DECISION

"MAKE A QUALITY DECISION"

Okay for those skeptic s that are reading this and saying, what a bunch of bull. You definitely need to keep reading. How do you expect to be happy, if you don't believe in yourself? You have a great business idea, but you don't do anything about it. Believe in yourself or that you can accomplish it. Sometimes you have to step out on faith. I did. Don't doubt. Doubt is discouraging it is unbelief, it is fear. Doubt will keeping you from making the right decision to live a happy life. Make a quality decision about what it is that you want to make you happy. Don't doubt yourself and say I can't do it. How do you know if you don't try? The soul surfer, Bethany Hamilton, didn't stop surfing after she lost her arm via shark attack. Bethany knew what she wanted. She believed in herself. She didn't doubt and made a decision that she was going to do what makes her happy. The track star, Oscar Pistoruis, didn't stop running track because he didn't have any legs. Another example; Martin Luther King Jr., did not stop fighting for Civil rights, because he thought

Farrah D. McBride

it wouldn't happen. He had a dream, a vision, about the future. He made it known. Martin believed in his dream and made a quality to decision to see that dream come to pass. Although his death was untimely, we are reaping the benefits of his desire, his belief and his quality decision.

EVALUATE/EXERCISE

"IF IT'S NOT WORKING FOR YOU GET RID OF IT"

Take a moment when you can and make a list of everything in your life that is not making you happy. Over the next few days, evaluate everything the list. After evaluating it, ask yourself to do I this is my life? How is it benefiting me? How is it building me up? What would it cost me to remove it out of my life? Would I remain unhappy? If you don't need it, get rid of it. None one wants to carry a bunch of unnecessary junk on their shoulders.

Exercise, yes exercise. Did I lose you with that? I need to exercise more regularly. Regular exercise promotes good health and overall wellness. You look better and you feel better. You ever want to go outside and play with your children and can't because you are overweight or unfit and get tired too easy. I am guilty again. Many of us are not happy with our weight and the way we look it. Tell yourself that you want to lose the weight, believe that you can and make a quality decision to do what is necessary to get you the results you desire.

FAITH/FEAR

"FEAR IS FAILURE BECAUSE YOU DIDN'T TRY"

Fear is the opposite of faith. Faith is believing in the unknown. It is believing that what you don't see exists. Fear is doubt, disbelief. It is the thought that you can't have something or do something because you don't believe in yourself. Fear is being afraid to fail. In life you will fail at something's and succeed at others. If you are unhappy in your current situation and do not step out on faith, you are letting fear control you. Have you ever had an idea or passion about something and wanted to try it, but didn't? You were afraid that it wouldn't work. How do know if you don't try? I am sure many of us have sat on our couch with a blanket and said, it would be nice if I had a place to put my arms. You may have thought of it but thought it was a dumb idea. That was until you saw it invented. Today Snuggle blankets are sold in places like Bed Bath and Beyond and Overstock.com. If you thought of it, but didn't act on it because of fear, you were probably shocked to see the idea actually was profitable and was kicking yourself about why you didn't try. Don't let fear keep of failing keep you pursing you passion. Don't let the fear of failure keep you from ultimately achieving success.

Unforgiveness can also keep you from being happy. That's right it can. Some people think that there is nothing wrong with holding a grudge. I'm here to tell you there is something wrong. When someone or something's make us angry, people at times have a tendency not to let that go. You think about it often and when something similar happens you get even more and more upset. You are now angry at the person or satiation who has wronged you. You then take it out on everyone else. Other people are clueless as to why you are so angry, mean, obnoxious and so unhappy. The only person to answer that is you. One thing that is certain, you are letting whether person, or situation continue to control you. Your unforgiveness or inability to forgive is giving power to an unnecessary person or situation. This will keep you from being happy. The individual you are angry with may not even know or care that you are mad. Chose to forgive them so that you can be happy.

Faith and Fear can't operate simultaneously. You can't want something and be afraid to go after what you want. I am a strong believe it having what it is I say and having the faith to see it all the way through. If you think back I am sure you can find many situations where you had the desire to do something. You procrastinated to get it done. News flash procrastination is a sign of fear. We have all done it at some point in our lives. We are afraid to pursue our dreams because we don't have the faith that it is going to work. Faith without action is like wanting to cross the street, but not making movement toward it. It doesn't matter if you crawl, walk run, skip, hop catch a bus or cab. If you don't make a move you will never get to where you want to go.

GIVING/GRATITUDE

"BE THANKFUL FOR WHAT YOU HAVE."

Being thankful for what you have is an open door to happiness. If you are jealous of what someone else has, you will never appreciate what you have and will find yourself in misery. I have a friend that loves love, but was unhappy in her relationship. Mary was in a long distance relationship and was longing to have that closeness she saw in other couples. We would go out and she would see couples happily in love. She said she was happy for the couples, but would complain about how she wishes she had what they had. She would then become sad. Mary became bitter and jealous of a relationship that had nothing to do with her. It made hanging out with her challenging. She would murmur and complain. I would tell Mary that complaining about it was not going to change it. Mary would often go into depression as a result of her bitterness. All this was because she was jealous. Coveting over what someone else has will not only not change your current state of mind, but keep you in an unhappy state of mind.

HEALTH

"YOUR BODY IS A TEMPLE. TAKE CARE OF IT."

Where health is concerned, it is a given that if you feel good, you look good and when we feel good and look good we are generally happy. What you put inside your body can affect your health. Example if you keep feeding your body junk food. It is going to perform that way. You can't put diesel fuel in car that was not made for it. If you do this, you know that eventually it would ruin the car inside and out. Now by no means am I a health nut, but I do try to eat healthy and watch what I put in my body. Do what is necessary to keep your body healthy. It would make you happier and your body will appreciate it.

INDEPENDENCE

"BEING INDEPENDENT DOESN'T MEAN YOU'RE LONELY"

It is okay to be dependent on someone for some things, but you need to make sure you are able to stand on your own. Be yourself and not who your friends or who people say you should be. If you are in a room with a whole bunch of your friends, do you find yourself doing what they want you to do? Are you finding yourself miserable? Go out and do stuff on your own, if it makes you happy. Be able to be alone, so you can be happy with your own company.

JUDGMENT

"DON'T BE SO QUICK TO JUDGE"

So many times we find ourselves judging people, based on their past, their current situation or what we think that they might do. In doing so is that really making you happy? I believe that you should be cautious, but don't judge someone based on your pre conceived thoughts about that person. A lot of times when you judge someone, you notice something about the person that is already in you, so when you think about it you may be judging yourself.

KINDNESS

"BEING KIND DOES NOT MAKE YOU NAÏVE."

Being kind sounds touché for most people. Kindness has a way of making things better and putting smiles of those your encounter and yourself. If you meet someone, who is unkind and has a negative attitude it's clear that they are not happy. Don't allow yourself to be pulled in there negativity and cause you to be unhappy. You can be kind, gentle and smile and keep your joy. I stress at work sometimes, I get sad and upset, but that rarely shows. When you see me, I am always smiling. People have taken noticed and commented my joyful nature. "You are so nice ,so giving and your always smiling. "You are happy even when you are tired." That's because I know my ABC's keep reading. You will get there. It is elementary.

LOVE

"LOVE IS A CHOICE"

Love is the most precious thing that anyone can ever receive and give. For the people who think that no one loves them, believe I know someone who does and will love you no matter what. If you really want to know, just ask the right person and your life will change. You will find a love that captivate your heart and transform your mind and soul. Love is precious, but it can also be tricky, treacherous and dangerous when given to the wrong person. I have a saying that you can't choose who you love, but you choose who you give your heart to. If who or what you love is not making you happy, it's a clear sign that you need to let it go. I was in a relationship with someone who I loved; the person didn't love me the way that I loved them. I went to bed crying many nights trying to understand, why I even loved this person. One morning, I woke up one morning and said, "I may love this person to the ends of the earth, but I am not

happy about how they are treating me and making me feel."
I chose to let go. If the person you love does not love you
and is not making you happy, you need to leave. Be happy
or miserable. The choice is yours.

MONEY

"MONEY IS A TOOL, USE IT WISELY"

For the love of money, people will lie, kill, steal and cheat. Money does make things happen, but if you don't control it, it will control you. Many people mismanage money. In most cases many of us live paycheck by paycheck. I am guilty of that. I have done it many times. The most important thing to know about money knows how to use it. It is a tool. You can never fix something properly if you don't have the right tools. There are a lot of resources out to help you figure out what to do to make your money work for you. What I am about to say next, my offend many, but I want you to think about what it is that I am about to say. A drug dealer knows how to turn $20 dollars into $100 dollars. Selling drugs is wrong, but the dealer used his money to make more money. Money is a resource. It is a tool. If you have any amount of it, you have the ability and the tool to make more of it.

NEVER GIVE UP

"NOTING WAS EVERY ACCOMPLISHED WITHOUT PERSISTENCE"

This is so important. Many of us have so many things that we want to do, so many desires and things that we let fall by the way side. We gave up or thought that whatever we were trying would not work. How do you know it wouldn't work? Did someone tell you it wasn't and you just believed it? Did you try? I have wanted to write since I was 8 years old. I am now 30 plus. It may have taken me over 20 years, but I never gave up. If I would have given up, you would not be reading this now. If I would have given up, I would not have been fulfilling my dream or my desire.

OPPORTUNITY

"OPPORTUNITIES PRESENT THEMSELVES EVERYDAY ARE YOU PREPARED?"

All an opportunity is an open door. It is an avenue to get you to the next level. Missing your opportunity could possible make you unhappy. Imagine you are working in an office and someone says, "This program would be better if it could do this." You know how to create it, but you say nothing. A few years later the program that you could have invented has now been built by someone else. It is now used in every office around the world. The Programmers net worth is over a billion dollars. You would probably be a bit upset and mad at yourself, because had you taken advantage of that opportunity, the billionaire could have been you. How many times, have you said of I can do this, but don't have a business card, portfolio or a website for people to take a look at your work. Every open door is not a good opportunity, you have to decide and know when it is right for you. In whatever the case is you need to be ready when the opportunity presents itself.

PRAISE/PRAY AND PLAY

"YOU HAVE TO DO SOMETHING TO GET SOMETHING."

I call this the 3Ps. You should always give thanks for what you do have and give praise to those who are worthy of it. It makes you happy and it makes them happy. If you are a supervisor or someone in management, you know that happy employees make a more productive and happier work environment. As a Christian, I believe in thanking God for everything that I have. I pray and then I play. What do I mean? Well I trust God as my source, I praise him, by thanking him and then I pray. I pray for myself, my, desires and I pray for others. The next them I do is a press play. Life is about action. Faith without works is dead. After I praise and pray, I press pray. It's like waiting to listen to your favorite Compact Disk (CD). You can say, I love this song. I can't wait to hear it and go on and on about it. Guess what you are not going to hear it until you press play. An action for your to get to the results you desired is required.

QUIET

"KNOW WHEN TO SPEAK"

Yes there are times where you must be silent and remain quiet to remain happy. Something's are not worth being said. There is a time and place for everything. Everything has a season. A lot of times when we are angry, we say things that we don't mean. Saying things when angry can destroy friendships and relationships. You have to know when to be heard and when to be quiet. Sometimes people will say and do stuff to get a response out of you. Sometimes it is more appropriate and will help you to maintain your happiness, if you say nothing. It will probably make them more upset. They will keep ranting and raving, take joy in knowing your silence is not making the situation worse.

RELATIONSHIPS

"SOME RELATIONSHIPS ARE MEANT FOR A LIFETIME OTHERS ARE MEANT FOR A SEASON"

Relationships are vital to everyone, but what is more important is having the right relationship. This includes romantic and platonic relationships. If you are in a relationship with someone who makes you feel bad or with someone who abuses you, hurts you or just makes your unhappy; leave. I know that that is easier said than done. Staying in unhealthy relationships do not help you grow or motivate you. It's actually quite the opposite. Relationships that make you unhappy causes stress, which can potentially lead to health problems. No one wants that, so cut the stress out of your life and allowing it access to make you unhappy.

SUBMISSION

"THERE IS FREEDOM IN SUBMISSION"

Yes submit. Did a lot of women just turned their heads and role their necks and say, hell to the no? I am not submitting to him. He doesn't do this or that. Men did you just say, yeah that's right she needs to submit to me? I am the head. WARNING! This is an emergency broadcast message from Ephesians 5:21(KJV). Submit yourselves to one another in the fear of God. Yes other verses do go on to say wives submit to your husband, but men it just doesn't stop there. Keep reading. Men also have a role in submission too. When I was in high school, I used to love the plays known to be written by William Shakespeare. One of my favorites is the Taming of the Shrew. It taught me, who actually benefits from submission. If you never read it, I suggest it. If you are a more visual person watch it on DVD. It will change your perspective. Submitting under authority can make you happy. It provides freedom, which you may not fully understand until you fully submit.

TONGUE

"CHOOSE YOUR WORDS WISELY"

The power of life and death is in the tongue. What you say can and will be held against you. I'm sure many of us have heard this. It is true. You have what you say. When you speak, you are give life to what you speak. So if you speak negatively, you are going to get negative results. Negativity stops movement, it stops growth. The words that you speak have the ability to change your surroundings. Everything that was created was created with words. The same thing that is used to create can be used to destroy. The key to being happy is watching what you say. Be mindful of what you allow people to say to you. If they are not positive words, they are not creating life. They are creating death on the inside. Eventually what is on the inside comes out. Again the power of life and death is in the tongue. You decide if you want to be happy, by what you allow come out of your mouth and those around you.

UNDERSTAND

"THINGS CHANGE AND PEOPLE CHANGE"

It's going to take understanding to be happy. You are going to have to understand that people in life, may not like you vice versa. You will sometimes have to agree to disagree. I used to hate this saying but it makes sense. You are going to have to agree to disagree. Value others opinion and don't take it personally. To be happy, understand you control your happiness and that no one else does. You decide your happiness.

VICTORY

"YOU CAN'T WHEN A BATTLE IF YOU ARE NOT WILLING TO FIGHT"

I am sure that everyone likes to win. No one likes to lose or feel like they have lost. You ever play your favorite video game and lost? You probably weren't too happy about it, but you kept playing and kept playing. You kept at it until you won the game. The disappointment you once felt turned into joy and victory, because you accomplished what you worked hard for. You didn't give up; you pushed through and received you desired results.

WISDOM

"SEEK WISDOM"

Wisdom is the principal thing. Wisdom is important to happiness, because if you make wise choices you are going to get better results. I told someone who was making poor choices and negative that ignorance is food for the foolish. If you want to be happy, you have to make wise decisions.

XENODOCHIAL-

"BE HOSPITABLE"

Xenodochial means to be nice and hospitable. It means to be kind and to be a servant. No not a slave. It means be willing to help and treat others with kindness. It follows the golden rule. Do unto others as you have them do unto you. There is a time to be nice and time to back away, but never a time when it is permissible to be rude. Being rude can lead to unhappiness. Example, you on your way to an interview you are running a little late. You get to the parking lot about 10 minutes before the interview starts. It's crowed. You are already frustrated that the traffic was crazy. You cut someone off in the parking lot because you don't see another available parking spot. You give the person the middle finger and head to your interview. When you arrive the reception says." Please have a seat in the back and wait, the person interviewing will be a little late." You get upset and sigh. You really need this job, so you calm down and apologize. When the manager arrives, she calls you in for the interview. To your surprise, the person interviewing you is the person you cut off and gave the middle finger. Your rudeness out in the parking lot, prevented you from getting the job. It would have been wise for you to remain calm in the parking lot. After all this the result of not using wisdom and being rude caused you unhappiness.

YOU

"YOU ARE THE KEY"

You are. You are the key to your happiness, not matter what day, no matter what the circumstance. You have the ability within yourself to make yourself happy and your happiness will affect those around you. The decisions you make will result in you being happy or unhappy. You have the power within yourself to change how you feel. You can change what you attract by what you radiate. If you radiate joy, happiness, love and peace you will attract it. Happy people want to be around other happy people.

ZEAL-

"BE PASSIONATE. FOLLOW YOUR DREAMS"

Be passionate about your hopes dreams and desires. Use your gifts and talents. These will make room for you. You love to bake, bake cookies and cake and sell them or start your own bakery. If you like doing hair, get your cosmetology license. If you like to sew and you are into fashion, design clothes. Whatever you are passionate about make it work for you. Let your gifts make room for you. Nothing makes a person happier than sharing a gift and seeing someone enjoy it.

The ABCs to happiness are elementary. Ask for what you want believe that you can have them. Care for the things that are important. Make quality decisions and don't doubt. Evaluate your life and exercise you mind body and soul. Have Faith. No need to Fear. Always be open to giving, because it would be a blessing to someone else. Try and stay in good health. Be independent, it's okay to be alone sometimes. Sometimes the happiest moments are the ones when you are alone, with you. Never judge be kind, love yourself, manage your money and never give up. Not all opportunities are bad, so be selective about the ones you take. Pray and always give praise, it brings you joy. Happiness is knowing when to be quiet, when to reconcile and maintain relationships with others. Be submitted to authority. Speak only those things that are going to edify and encourage someone, so that they may lifted up. Tame your tongue, be careful what you say and how you say it. The tongue can be a power weapon, use it wisely. It will bring you joy or pain. Try to understand others; don't be so quick to formulate opinions. You may miss out on what could be a benefit to you. Always know that you can always have victory and be virtuous. Wisdom is the principal thing. Know how to become wise. Stop making excuses. Know yourself. Be good to you. No one will ever treat you better than you treat yourself. People are going to treat you based on what you allow. If you are not good to you, they are not going to be good to you. Would that make you happy? Lastly be enthusiastic, about all things you want in life. I told you happiness is elementary.

ABOUT THE AUTHOR

I first recognized my creativity as a writer after winning an essay contest as child and being published in a local newspaper. It has been my dream to become a writer ever since. I was raised in single-family household with my three siblings in Augusta, Georgia. I left home at eighteen to serve my county. After several years in the service, I left to raise my son in Maryland, where I completed my bachelor's degree in health care administration and human resource management.

Printed in the United States
By Bookmasters